LISTENER'S G

Y0-DAM-680

In
CLASSICAL
mood

Tender Moments

Tender Moments

*S*ome of the greatest pieces ever inspired by the universal
emotion of love are represented in this volume. Intimacy
and tenderness, passion and joy—these are the feelings related to
matters of the heart that form the basis of a wealth of music.
Mimì's heartfelt aria "Mi chiamano Mimì" ("They call me Mimì")
from Puccini's *La Bohème* contrasts with the alluring false
sentiments of Mozart's wily hero from *Don Giovanni*. The sense
of sweet longing, so eloquently expressed in Shostakovich's
"Romance" complements the sighs of Elgar's *Sospiri*, while the
tragic love story of *Romeo and Juliet* is represented in two
contrasting forms: the yearning "Balcony Scene" from Prokofiev's
ballet, and Delius's dream-like "Walk to the Paradise Garden."

THE LISTENER'S GUIDE — WHAT THE SYMBOLS MEAN

THE COMPOSERS
Their lives... their loves..
their legacies...

THE MUSIC
Explanation... analysis...
interpretation...

THE INSPIRATION
How works of genius
came to be written

THE BACKGROUND
People, places, and events
linked to the music

Contents

ANTON RUBINSTEIN *1829–1894*

Two Melodies

OPUS 3, NO.1: MELODY IN F MAJOR

This gentle piano miniature conveys a delicate sentiment in the simplest possible way. The opening phrase gives it a shape that is followed and varied throughout, reflecting a sense of tender passion. The music does not build to a passionate climax, but instead expresses the delight of being close to a loved one. As a virtuoso pianist, Rubinstein played in many a concert hall, but this melody is more suitable for an intimate audience, to be shared in well-chosen company.

THE BROTHERS RUBINSTEIN

Anton Rubinstein (*left*) and his younger brother Nikolai were powerful musical figures in 19th-century Russia. Both were superbly gifted pianists, but it was Anton who became a legendary piano virtuoso. Both brothers toured Europe, giving concerts as child prodigies. At first, Nikolai studied medicine, while Anton struggled to survive as a music teacher in Vienna. Following a triumphant concert tour of Europe, Anton founded, and became director of, the St. Petersburg Conservatory of Music in 1862. Nikolai founded the Moscow Conservatory four years later and quickly became a popular figure in Moscow society. Although both brothers could be volatile teachers, they were greatly loved by their pupils—most notably Tchaikovsky, who was taught by Anton and became a colleague of Nikolai. Anton composed a large body of work, but is remembered mainly for his "Melody in F Major." Nikolai, on the other hand, wrote little, claiming that his brother wrote "enough for three." Keeping his appetite for the good life until the end, Nikolai called for a dozen oysters just before dying of consumption in Paris, in 1881, at age 45. Anton lived for another 13 years, and left a lasting legacy to musical education in Russia.

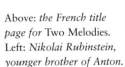

Above: *the French title page for* Two Melodies. Left: *Nikolai Rubinstein, younger brother of Anton.*

MOSCOW AND ST. PETERSBURG

 When the Rubinstein brothers became directors of the St. Petersburg and Moscow Conservatories, they found themselves involved in a rivalry between the two principal Russian cities. Peter the Great, who founded St. Petersburg in 1703, had a high regard for art, and within a century, his city had become the center of Russian cultural life. On the other hand, Moscow (*right*) was, for centuries, the spiritual center of Russia, clinging to ancient traditions. The city only

grew seriously both industrially and culturally from the mid-19th century, and it was not until after the 1917 Revolution that it became the capital. In 1859, Nikolai Rubinstein founded the Russian Music Society in Moscow, which had a radical effect on musical life in the city. Since the Conservatory opened in 1866, it has consistently produced outstanding musicians.

ONE-PIECE WONDERS

 Rubinstein is not the only composer who is known for just one work. Pietro Mascagni and Ruggero Leoncavallo are mainly known for their twin opera hits *Cavalleria rusticana* and *Pagliacci* (*left*) respectively, while Amilcare Ponchielli is remembered mainly for his opera *La Gioconda*, with its famous "Dance of the Hours" ballet.

KEY NOTES

 Polish pianist Arthur Rubinstein (no relation) was often confused with the composer of Melody in F Major. On his travels, ships' orchestras would strike up the tune, in misplaced homage, when he entered the salon. He soon gave up protesting, and just acknowledged the compliment.

SERGEI RACHMANINOV *1873–1943*

Fourteen Songs

OPUS 34, NO.14: VOCALISE

achmaninov initially wrote "Vocalise," or wordless song, for soprano and piano, and later arranged it for orchestra, as heard here. In the 19th century, a vocalise was merely an exercise for singers, designed to help produce a sustained, lyrical sound, or extend vocal technique. The idea of using the voice as a musical instrument, however, caught Rachmaninov's imagination, and his "Vocalise," with its tender mood of reflective solitude, is one of the most inspired of its kind.

MYSTERIOUS ADMIRER

In 1912 Rachmaninov received a letter from an admirer, identified only as "Re." He soon discovered that "Re" was poet Marietta Shaginian, and he asked her to suggest some poems for a set of songs. These formed the basis of the Opus 34 collection, of which only "Vocalise" is wordless.

KEY NOTES

Brazilian composer Heitor Villa-Lobos's vocalise rivals Rachmaninov's in popularity. The most famous of his Bachianas Brasileiras is No.5, which is scored for a soprano voice and eight cellos.

GIACOMO PUCCINI *1858–1924*

La Bohème

MI CHIAMANO MIMÌ

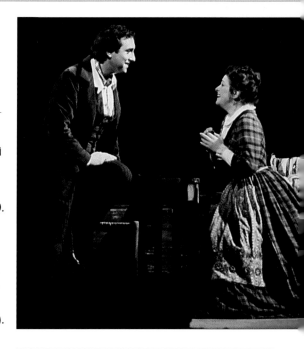

*I*t is Christmas Eve, about 1830. In a poor artist's garret at the top of a house in Paris, a frail young seamstress calls to ask for a light for her candle. Rodolfo, a poet, answers the door and is immediately charmed by his visitor. She introduces herself: "Mi chiamano Mimì" ("They call me Mimì"). She embroiders artificial flowers for a living, but it is nature's flowers that she loves. The piece starts simply enough, but becomes more passionate as she looks forward to seeing the flowers of spring, and the music betrays her first tender feelings for this friendly young man. After its emotional climax, she trails off: "I wouldn't know what else to tell you about myself," ending as simply and modestly as she began.

BIRTH OF THE BOHEMIAN

La Bohème is based on the book *Scènes de la vie de Bohème* written by Henri Mürger in 1854. Although he was a mediocre writer, Mürger's descriptions of Parisian life were highly successful, and he later adapted them as a play. He and Puccini have helped to define the popular image of bohemian life—impoverished artists freezing in rickety garrets.

ART, LIFE AND DEATH

The plot of *La Bohème* is fairly simple. It concerns two women, frail Mimì and irrepressible Musetta, and four young men who share a garret: the poet Rodolfo, the painter Marcello, the musician Schaunard and the philosopher Colline. Impoverished as they are, they all enjoy Christmas Eve at a café—at the expense of Alcindoro, a rich, old suitor of Musetta, Marcello's mistress. From here the story darkens. Racked by consumption, Mimì is tormented by Rodolfo's quarreling and jealous suspicions. She later finds out that, knowing of her illness, he wants to spare her the discomfort of sharing his unheated lodgings. The four friends scrape together money for a doctor for Mimì, but they are too late. She quietly passes away, and the opera ends on Rodolfo's heartbroken cries.

Characters from La Bohème *toast the memory of the librettist, Henri Mürger.*

HELPLESS HEROINES

Puccini's heroines tend to fall into two camps: Either they are powerful and resourceful or, like the consumptive Mimì, tragic victims. The slave girl Liù in *Turandot*, is another example—she sacrifices herself for love of her master, Calaf. Cio Cio San, the heroine of *Madame Butterfly* (*left*), takes her own life when she is betrayed by her feckless American husband.

ITALIAN RIVALRY

 In 1893, Puccini's compatriot, Ruggero Leoncavallo (*below*) also announced plans to set Mürger's *Bohemian Scenes* to music. Leoncavallo, composer of the opera *Pagliacci*, produced his *La Bohème* in 1897, a year after Puccini's. The two are striking in their similarities— and differences. Like Puccini, Leoncavallo devotes the first two acts to the lighter side of bohemian life, which later develops into something darker. Although his music is good, Leoncavallo's *La Bohème* can't match the genius of Puccini's and is now merely an interesting curiosity.

REVOLUTIONARY YEARS

 La Bohème is set in 1830s Paris. By this time, France had endured over 40 years of extraordinary turbulence. The French Revolution, which began in Paris in 1789, was followed by the rise of Napoleon Bonaparte, who went on to conquer half of Europe before being defeated in 1815 at Waterloo. Fifteen years later, France once again saw revolutionary activity. Rising unemployment and inflation led to civil unrest, and in July 1830, there was bitter fighting in Paris (*above*). The storming of public buildings led to barricades being built all over the city, and culminated in the abdication of King Charles X.

KEY NOTES

 Puccini first visited England in April 1897, when he arrived in Manchester for the premiere of La Bohème. *Unimpressed, he called Manchester a "land of black smoke, darkness, cold, rain, cotton and fog. A veritable inferno! A horrible place to stay!"*

ERIK SATIE *1866–1925*

Café-concert Songs

JE TE VEUX

*H*eard here in a piano version, this wistful little waltz, "I want you," was originally written for voice and piano. It dates to around 1900, when Satie was eking out a living as a cabaret pianist in Montmartre, Paris. It is one of several songs he wrote for music-hall star Paulette Darty, known as the "Queen of the Slow Waltz." For the most part, it has a tender, melancholic feel, expressing bittersweet desire.

SWINGING CATS

Cabaret is entertainment provided in night club or bar. Although it is often associated with Germany in the 1930s and its decadent overtones, it began in Paris in the early 1900s. Its birthplace was the *Chat Noir* ("The Black Cat"), a Parisian bar frequented by poets, artists, and musicians, including Satie.

KEY NOTES

Satie once visited Paulette Darty with his publisher, Jean Belton. Darty was in the bath, and heard Belton sing "Je te veux." The song had "such charm and such an attractive quality, I quickly got out of my bath to express my enchantment," she said.

RICHARD STRAUSS *1864–1949*

Don Quixote

OPUS 35: DIALOGUE BETWEEN THE KNIGHT AND SERVANT

*T*his is one of a series of tone poems that display Strauss's superb mastery of the orchestra and his ability to tell stories through music. *Don Quixote* comprises a theme with ten variations, each describing one of the adventures of the eccentric Don and his trusty servant Sancho Panza. This, an excerpt from the third variation, is in two parts. In the second half, heard here, the knight launches into ecstatic reveries, in which he muses on the glories of chivalry and dreams of his beloved, the idealized Dulcinea. The variation passes its noble, sinuous theme from one instrument to another, building in intensity. This is replaced by the melody of the lovely Dulcinea herself, as the Don contemplates her with great tenderness.

The Man of La Mancha

Published in 1605, Miguel de Cervantes's classic *Don Quixote de la Mancha*, tells of an old man who believes that he is a knight errant. With his squire Sancho Panza, who rides on a donkey, he sets out to find glory on behalf of the beautiful Dulcinea. Quixote (*left*) dreams of chivalry, but his adventures only provide merriment for onlookers. He attacks windmills (*right*),

believing they are giants and charges an "army" of sheep. At another time, he and Panza ride a wooden horse and believe they are flying. Finally, to rescue Quixote from his delusions, a friend disguised as a knight challenges and defeats him. The ruse works, and Quixote lays down his arms. Some time later, he dies.

Instruments as Characters

Throughout *Don Quixote*, Strauss's two main characters are represented by solo instruments. Quixote is represented by the cello and Sancho Panza mostly by the viola—although the tenor tuba and bass clarinet also take on the role. In this way, the two men can be clearly identified against the orchestral background, and are made vivid and colorful. In *Ein Heldenleben* ("A Hero's Life"), where Strauss gives himself the role of hero, he used this technique again, using the solo violin to portray his wife.

Pauline de Ahna, Strauss's wife, was represented musically in his work.

Best-selling Author

Miguel de Cervantes (*left*), the author of *Don Quixote de la Mancha*, was born in 1547 in Alcalá, near Madrid, Spain. A man of action, he lost the use of a hand in the great 1571 naval battle of Lepanto. While on active service, he was captured by pirates, and spent five years imprisoned in Algiers. Cervantes wrote many plays—now mostly lost—but to make money, worked as a tax collector. He was jailed for financial bungling and, according to tradition, this allowed him to write the first part of *Don Quixote*, published in 1605. Although it became one of the best-loved classics ever (its sales are second only to the Bible), it did not make him rich. Cervantes later joined a Franciscan order, continuing to write plays, stories, and poems. He died of edema in 1616.

Strauss the Conductor

Richard Strauss (*right*) was a noted conductor, and not just of his own works. He became assistant conductor to the great Hans von Bülow at Meiningen when he was only 21, and went on to excel on the concert platform and in the opera pit. In 1898 he became chief conductor of the Royal Court Opera in Berlin, where he championed new music, including Elgar's. Known for his restrained podium manner, Strauss once advised would-be conductors that the thumb of the left hand should never leave the waistcoat pocket.

KEY NOTES

Despite his undoubted brilliance and success, Strauss was modest about his abilities. While rehearsing his music in London he said to the orchestra, "I know what I want, and I know what I meant when I wrote this. After all, I may not be a first-rate composer, but I am a first-class, second-rate composer."

FRÉDÉRIC CHOPIN *1810–1849*

Fantaisie-impromptu in C-sharp Minor

OPUS 66

This piece demonstrates the poetic fire combined with sensitivity that won Chopin such acclaim. The composer called it *Impromptu*, but his editor Julius Fontana added the prefix "Fantaisie," to suggest contrasting moods. It is in three parts: the outer two, with their torrents of notes, betray a turbulent spirit. In complete contrast, a heartfelt melody breaks through in the central section, appearing rather like a gentle rainbow crowning a rugged landscape.

FANTAISIE AND IMPROMPTU

The impromptu, invented in the 19th century, is a work, usually for the piano, which is meant to sound as if it were written on the spur of the moment.

KEY NOTES

*The melody of **Fantaisie-impromptu** was one of the first classical tunes to be adapted for a popular song. In 1918, Harry Carroll and Joseph McCarthy used it for their song "I'm Always Chasing Rainbows."*

13

SIR EDWARD ELGAR *1857–1934*

Sospiri

OPUS 70

lthough he is often depicted as the quintessential Englishman, Elgar had a great love of Italy, and had already depicted the glory of its landscape and history in his overture *In the South (Alassio)*. *Sospiri* ("Sighs") written in 1914, on the eve of World War I, is another of his Italianate pieces. It is scored for strings, harp, and organ. Small forces perhaps, but ideal for this quiet, sad piece. In it he creates an atmosphere of great longing and regret, and of a deep sorrow, which could both reflect the anguish of love and foreshadow the loss of an idyllic world about to be destroyed by war.

ELGAR'S WAR EFFORT

Although Elgar was depressed by the outbreak of World War I in 1914, he wanted to do his part to help, and enlisted as a police inspector (*below, left in front*) in Hampstead, North London. According to his friend W.H. Reed, Elgar eagerly dressed up in his armband, belt, and hat. He also carried a truncheon, which he is said to have "handled rather gingerly." He resigned the following year, but then joined the Hampstead Volunteer Reserve. Despite the war, he managed to produce *The Spirit of England* in 1915, a setting of three poems by Laurence Binyon (1869–1943). These include the famous "For the Fallen," which is forever linked with World War I, and contains: "They shall grow not old, as we that are left grow old."

ELGAR'S ENEMIES

Although he was a highly respected composer, Elgar had his share of detractors by the time he wrote *Sospiri*. Chief of these was Charles Villiers Stanford (*right*), a successful composer himself and a highly influential figure in British music. During the war, he produced *A History of Music* in which he described Elgar as an imitator who "reaped where others had sown." Although Elgar's supporters were quick to defend him, Stanford's poisonous judgement was passed on to his Cambridge pupils, including Ralph Vaughan Williams.

KEY NOTES

Elgar dedicated Sospiri to violinist W.H. Reed. Founder of the London Symphony Orchestra, Reed gave the first performances of Elgar's late chamber music works, including the Violin Sonata. He also wrote two books on the composer.

FRANZ SCHUBERT *1797–1828*

Schwanengesang

D957, NO.4: STÄNDCHEN

Schubert's "Ständchen" or "Serenade," is one of a cycle of 14 songs known as *Schwanengesang* ("Swan Song"), issued by music publisher Tobias Haslinger after the composer's death. The melody is simplicity itself, consisting of a repeated yearning phrase. But behind this apparent naiveté is the subtle vocal writing of which Schubert was such a master. Its declarations of love are earnest, and have a bittersweet quality that sets the serenade apart from most. At times, the piece becomes quite passionate, but it retains an underlying serenity, with the piano mimicking the mandolin, the classic instrument of the serenade.

THE DEATH OF SCHUBERT

At the end of October 1828, Schubert complained of sickness after eating fish. From then on, he ate nothing, was confined to his room, and suffered delirium, during which he sang constantly. On November 19, he uttered his final words, "Here, here is my end," and then passed away. His death certificate gave the cause of death as *Nervenfieber*—an imprecise term thought to mean typhoid fever. Recently it has been suggested that this could also refer to syphilis, which is consistent with a diagnosis of "advanced disintegration of the blood corpuscles" just prior to death. It could also explain the onset of his final sickness, due not to food poisoning from fish but to mercury poisoning. Mercury was the standard medication for syphilis, and one of his doctors, Josef von Vering, was an expert on its treatment.

Franz Schubert's tomb in the musicians' section of Vienna's Central Cemetery.

"STÄNDCHEN" VIA BEETHOVEN

The poem "Ständchen" was written by Ludwig Rellstab. He sent it with six others to Beethoven (*left*), but was amazed to get them back from Schubert, already set to music. Some of the poems bore Beethoven's pencil marks: The master had liked these best but, too ill to compose himself, passed them on to Schubert.

SERGEI PROKOFIEV *1891–1953*

Romeo and Juliet

SUITE NO. 1, OPUS 64A: BALCONY SCENE

Prokofiev's music here portrays one of Shakespeare's most famous scenes, which begins with Romeo's "But soft! what light through yonder window breaks?" Shimmering chords and high violin notes evoke an enchanted moonlit night. Then earthier interruptions from lower wind and brass instruments give way to a luscious melody, with swooping horns and cellos, as Romeo's love pours forth. The music becomes urgent and stormy— reflecting the doomed lovers' fate—before returning to the tender ecstasies of the opening, and ending peacefully.

PIANO PIECES

As with all ballet music, a piano version of *Romeo and Juliet* was prepared as a rehearsal score for the dancers. Prokofiev later turned some of it into a concert work for piano: his *Ten Pieces from Romeo and Juliet, Opus 75.*

KEY NOTES

Referring to the difficulties in getting the ballet performed, Galina Ulanova—who danced Juliet—proposed a toast at its Moscow premiere, "Never was a tale of greater woe/Than Prokofiev's music to Romeo!"

CAMILLE SAINT-SAËNS *1835–1921*

Romance for Flute
in D-flat Major

OPUS 37

Saint-Saëns wrote this *Romance* in 1871, during the period known as the "silver age" of French flute playing. Improvements in flute design made the instrument more expressive, and players adopted a playing style modeled on the human voice. The *Romance* is purely melodic, free from the virtuoso flamboyance of later 19th-century solo instrumental music. It is mostly gentle and warm, and conveys a touching sense of intimacy through its use of the lower, "breathy," register of the flute.

FLAUTIST'S FAVORITE

Saint-Saëns dedicated *Romance* to composer and flautist Paul Taffanel. It became a favorite of Taffanel, who is regarded as the father of the modern French school of flute playing.

KEY NOTES

Saint-Saëns could write quickly and effortlessly. He wrote his Piano Concerto No.2 *in only 17 days.*

DMITRI SHOSTAKOVICH *1906–1975*

The Gadfly

OPUS 97: ROMANCE

*S*hostakovich's 20th-century romance is a far cry from the dainty versions written in the 18th and 19th centuries. He wrote it as part of the incidental music for the 1955 Soviet movie *The Gadfly* ("Ovod"). Based on a novel by E.L. Voynich, the film centers on the adventures of an Italian freedom fighter during Austrian domination in the 19th century—the Gadfly of the title, whose "sting" maddens the foreign occupiers. Although our hero meets a tragic end in front of a firing squad, he has many romantic adventures along the way, captured here in the beautiful melody. It swoops in an eloquent expression of tender sentiment. The theme is taken first by a solo violin, played over the simplest of accompaniments. It climbs with increasing ardor, before giving way to a darker, more urgent middle section. Finally the full orchestral strings pick up the melody and bring the piece to its wistful close.

SOVIET LIGHT MUSIC

The Gadfly was one of more than 35 films for which Shostakovich wrote the music. As with many other composers, film

scores provided a welcome source of income. In the Soviet Union they were also proof of his willingness to use art to entertain the masses, as any attempt at high-brow art could severely damage an artist's career. Shostakovich fell in bad favor with the authorities several times, but the light, "acceptable" music that he produced may not

A 1951 Soviet film in the making.

have been intended solely to please the state, for he genuinely enjoyed popular music. In 1928, he produced an orchestration of *Tahiti Trot*—better known as "Tea for Two," and he also wrote two suites for jazz orchestra. His habitual unhappy expression belied his sense of humor: He called one of his songs, for bass and piano, "Preface to the Complete Edition of My Thoughts and Works about this Preface."

LIKE FATHER...

One of the most compelling interpreters of Shostakovich's music is his own son Maxim (*below, right, with his father*). Maxim won a place at the Moscow Conservatory by performing his father's *Piano Concerto No.2 in F Major*, and went on to become a distinguished conductor, working with the Moscow Philharmonic Orchestra and the U.S.S.R. State Symphony Orchestra. He is also a successful opera conductor, and has performed on many recordings of his father's works, including this one.

KEY NOTES

After composing the score for The Gadfly, *Shostakovich went to care for his ailing mother in Komarovo, where he did little writing. She died a few months later on November 9, 1955.*

WOLFGANG AMADEUS MOZART
1756–1791

Don Giovanni

K527: LÀ CI DAREM LA MANO

In this duet from *Don Giovanni*, the hero does what he enjoys most— seducing a young woman. Here, it is Zerlina, a peasant girl, on her wedding day! The groom is conveniently removed from the scene, and Don Giovanni moves in, urging her to come with him to his country house. This appears as a tender scene, as the Don offers Zerlina wealth and happiness to a beguiling melody: "*Là ci darem la mano*" ("There we will give each other our hands"). Wary of his enticements, Zerlina sings, "I want to and yet I don't." He persists, and she protests feebly that her heart bleeds for her fiancé, whom she has left behind. But she is persuaded and nearly gives in. Mozart's music demonstrates an artless simplicity, yet it is subtle and masterly: Beneath the talk of marriage and wealth burn feelings more urgent and carnal.

THE UNREPENTANT ROGUE

 This opera, whose full title is *Il dissoluto punito, ossia Il Don Giovanni* ("The Rake Punished, or Don Giovanni"), is one of the many musical retellings of the legend of Don Juan, the amorous, depraved adventurer. His exploits include disguising himself to ravish a woman, and mortally wounding her father when challenged; pretending to marry another; almost luring a young peasant bride away from her groom; and escaping an awkward situation by disguising himself as his manservant—who has to endure the beating meant for his master. In a cemetery, Don Giovanni encounters a statue of the man he killed, and invites it to dinner. The statue arrives at his house, and the unrepentant rogue meets an untimely end as the stone "guest" drags him down to Hell.

THE DON JUAN LEGEND

Don Juan first appeared in a play *El Burlador de Sevilla*, written by a 17th–century Spanish monk, Tirso de Molina. It was subsequently rewritten many times, both as a play by Molière and a ballet by Gluck. In all its various forms, two elements remain consistent: the lecherous exploits of Don Giovanni and the statue which comes to life (*left*) and brings about divine retribution.

KEY NOTES

 Librettist Lorenzo da Ponte wrote the text for Don Giovanni while working on two other operas. He wrote for 12 hours a day, a bottle of wine in one hand and a box of tobacco in the other. And he also found distraction in the arms of his landlord's daughter.

FREDERICK DELIUS *1862–1934*

A Village Romeo and Juliet

THE WALK TO THE PARADISE GARDEN

*I*n this interlude, which contains the most famous music from the opera, the lovers Sali and Vreli are trying to find a place where they will not be recognized. Having just left a fair where they were spotted, they are on their way to the Paradise Garden—a run-down riverside inn where they can dance. The music has a haunting, timeless quality to it, full of loving tenderness but also of sad resignation and occasional outbursts of passion. The writing for orchestra is exquisite, with its plaintive wind solos weaving over delicate strings. A melody begins to take shape. At first it is only in fragments, but these are gradually drawn together until the tune is played by the full orchestra, reaching an emotionally overwhelming climax.

THE LIBRETTOS

A Village Romeo and Juliet is based on a short story in German by Gottfried Keller. After trying three librettos, Delius failed to find one that suited him, and wrote the words himself in 1899.

A Village Romeo and Juliet

The opera, set in Switzerland, tells of the doomed love of Sali and Vreli, whose feuding fathers forbid them to meet. The story is overshadowed by a character known as the Dark Fiddler, who warns the young couple of misfortunes that are liable to befall their families. Sali and Vreli's efforts to make a life together are foiled by constant family feuding and gossip. One day the couple go to the fair in Berghald, and on to the Paradise Garden, in order to be alone. But again they meet the Dark Fiddler. In despair they take to the river in a hay barge and remove the bung. They cling to each other as the boat slowly sinks.

Delius and Fenby

In his later years, when blind and paralyzed, Delius relied on the help of Eric Fenby. Born in 1906, Fenby (*below*) was a composer himself, and became adviser to music publishers Boosey & Hawkes, and professor at London's Royal Academy of Music. His works include the overture *Rossini on Ilkley Moor*, and many film scores. His book *Delius as I Knew Him* became a classic. He died in 1997.

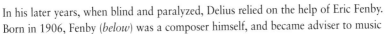

Key Notes

The relationship between Delius and Fenby was the subject of Ken Russell's acclaimed television drama Song of Summer, which featured Max Adrian as the old composer and Christopher Gable as Fenby.

Credits & Acknowledgments

Picture Credits

Cover /Title and Contents Pages/ IBC: SuperStock AKG London: 3(br & l), 7(bl), 8(r), (Gustav Klimt: Schubert at the Piano) 16, 23(bl), Eric Lessing 17(tr); Bridgeman Art Library, London/Stapleton Collection (Karl Schweninger: The Duet) 2, Giraudon (French School: The Charter or Death, July 1830) 8(tl), Victoria & Albert Museum, London (Henri de Toulouse-Lautrec: Mlle. Marcelle Lender) 9, Giraudon/Musée D'Orsay, Paris (John Singer Sargent: Carmencita) 10, Bonhams, London (Francisco J. Torrome: Don Quixote & the Windmill) 11(cr), Private Collection (Sir John Everett Millais: "Yes or No?") 14, Agnew & Sons, London (John Francis Rigaud: Romeo & Juliet) 18, Josef Mensing Gallery, Hamm-Rhynern (Julius Kockert: Dusk) 24; Corbis/Bettmann 11(bl); James Davis Travel Photography: 20; The Elgar Foundation: 15(bl); Mary Evans Picture Library: 7(tr), 11(tl), 12(tl & bc), 15(r), 17(bl), 23(r); Fine Art Photographic Library/Private Collection (Edward Killingworth Johnson: The Old Home) 5; Getty Images: 19, 25(tr); Lebrecht Collection: 3(bc), (Bella Manyevich: Snow Scene in Moscow) 4(tr); Novosti (London): 21(r); Performing Arts Library/Clive Barda 4(b), 22; Society for Cooperation in Russian & Soviet Studies: 21(l); The Stock Market: 13; Universal Pictorial Press & Agency Ltd: 25(bl); Reg Wilson: 6

All illustrations and symbols: John See